Low-calorie Cottage Cheese Cookbook

Table of Contents

Introduction

The world of low-calorie cottage cheese dishes stands out as a delicious and nourishing fusion in a culinary environment where flavor and health are frequently seen as being at conflict. Those looking to maintain or lose weight without sacrificing flavor appreciate cottage cheese, a versatile dairy product with a texture similar to curd. This article explores low-calorie cottage cheese recipes and reveals all the health advantages they provide.

Cottage cheese is a nutritional powerhouse.

Because of its well-known high protein content, cottage cheese is a great food choice for people trying to gain and keep lean muscle mass. Protein provides feelings of fullness and contentment, which helps to reduce cravings and avoid overeating. It also stimulates the building of muscles. In addition, cottage cheese contains many important nutrients, including phosphorus, selenium, and vitamin B12, and is a great source of calcium, which helps to maintain strong bones and teeth.

Weight Loss Done Deliciously:

Low-calorie cottage cheese recipes' capacity to support weight management objectives while providing a pleasurable culinary experience is one of their most alluring features. Cottage cheese contributes to a feeling of fullness and satiety by having high protein content and a low calorie count, which helps prevent consuming too many calories during the day. It is simpler to stick to a healthy eating plan when cottage cheese is used in a variety of recipes because it adds a creamy and hearty aspect that heightens the sense of enjoyment.

Blood Sugar and Energy Levels in Balance:

Protein and good fats found in cottage cheese can help control blood sugar levels. Cottage cheese slows down the digestion of carbs when it is ingested with a meal or as a snack, minimizing sharp rises and falls in blood sugar levels. As a result, energy levels are maintained and cravings for processed or sugary foods are decreased, providing consistent energy throughout the day.

Promoting muscle repair and recovery:

Casein protein, a slow digesting protein found in cottage cheese, promotes a steady flow of amino acids into the bloodstream. Because it promotes long-term muscle growth and regeneration, cottage cheese is a great choice for post workout recovery. Numerous low-calorie cottage cheese dishes can be enjoyed as post workout meals to make sure the body gets the nutrients it needs for a speedy recovery.

Redefining Versatility:

Low-calorie cottage cheese dishes are appealing because of how adaptable they are. Easily incorporated into both savory and sweet recipes, cottage cheese enables a wide variety of culinary creations. The options are endless, ranging from savory cottage cheese stuffed mushrooms to protein rich morning parfaits. Because cottage cheese is so adaptable, people who follow various dietary preferences and constraints can take advantage of its health benefits in ways that appeal to them.

Improvement of Digestive Health:

Probiotics, which are helpful microorganisms that support a healthy gut microbiota, are present in cottage cheese. For proper digestion, nutritional assimilation, and immune system operation, a healthy gut flora is essential. Including cottage cheese in one's diet helps support a healthy gut ecosystem, enhancing digestion and general wellbeing.

Low-calorie cottage cheese dishes offer a delicious and healthy combination. Cottage cheese has an exceptional nutritional profile that includes a high protein content, necessary nutrients, and gut friendly bacteria.

As a result, it offers several health advantages that support a range of wellness objectives.

The variety of low-calorie cottage cheese recipes allows you to discover a world where nourishment and enjoyment coexist, whether you're trying to lose weight, want to increase your protein consumption, or are just looking to enjoy delicious and nutritious meals.

Cottage Cheese: The Art of Low-calorie Cooking

The art of low-calorie cooking with cottage cheese stands out as a masterpiece in the world of culinary exploration because it honors both flavor and nutrition. Cottage cheese offers a wide range of culinary options for developing mouthwatering dishes that satisfy the palate while adhering to health conscious objectives thanks to its creamy texture and faint tang. A careful balancing of methods and ingredients is required for this complex synthesis of flavor and wellness, creating a symphony of culinary delights that reinterpret the meaning of indulgence.

The Potential of Cottage Cheese:
Understanding the inherent features of the food is the first step in learning the skill of cooking with cottage cheese that is low in calories. Cottage cheese is the perfect base for creating wholesome but tasty dishes because of its high protein level and low fat content. However, the texture's minor graininess can present both a problem and a chance. Here is where culinary ingenuity shines, upgrading this plain dairy product into a versatile element that may enhance a variety of cuisines.

Techniques:

Blending, straining, and pairing

Low-calorie cottage cheese recipes are built on the principles of blending, straining, and pairing. Using these methods, professionals and amateur cooks can take use of cottage cheese's special qualities to produce dishes that will astound the palate.

1. Blending: By blending cottage cheese, you may smooth down its texture and easily incorporate it into sauces, dips, and smoothies. It produces a velvety smoothness that gives food body and creaminess without using heavy cream or other high fat ingredients.

2. Straining: Straining cottage cheese reduces the amount of liquid, creating a rich and opulent base. This method is very helpful for producing creamy cheesecakes, spreads, and rich toppings that are low in calories while providing a decadent experience.

3. Pairing: To improve the flavor and nutritional profile of cottage cheese, pairing is the art of combining it with complementary products. It adds a delicious diversity of textures and is enriched with vitamins, minerals, and dietary fiber when blended with fresh herbs, fruits, nuts, and whole grains.

Brilliant Breakfast:

The first meal of the day, breakfast, offers a superb blank slate for the art of low-calorie cottage cheese cookery. Breakfast staples like pancakes, waffles, and oatmeal are given a touch of protein and smoothness by the addition of cottage cheese, making them into gratifying and fulfilling feasts. Creamy cottage cheese can be blended with colorful fruits and crunchy granola to make a parfait that is both beautiful to look at and delicious to eat.

Delicious Sensations:

Cottage cheese is cleverly used into savory meals to give them a new level of excellence. Its mild flavor blends seamlessly into a wide range of dishes, from frittatas with vegetable studded to stuffed mushrooms and spinach quiches. While keeping a low-calorie profile, the richness of blended cottage cheese may also be used to make decadent pasta sauces that envelop each strand of pasta in a velvety embrace.

Decadent Desserts, Guilt Free:

When it comes to cottage cheese based low-calorie cookery, desserts become a blank canvas for creativity. Cottage cheese contributes its creaminess to make decadent desserts that are both gratifying and healthy, from light cheesecakes to luscious mousse. Natural sweeteners, fragrant extracts, and cottage cheese are blended to create a guilt free dessert that is good for both the taste buds and the waistline.

Taste and Wellness in Balance:

The skill of low-calorie cooking with cottage cheese demonstrates how flavor and health may coexist without conflict. Chefs and ordinary cooks alike discover a world where culinary creativity and nutritional sense converge as they experiment with blending, straining, and combining. Cooking with low-calorie cottage cheese is an excellent example of how to make delectable foods while keeping your health in mind.

In this culinary creation, cottage cheese goes beyond its role as an ordinary ingredient to become a blank canvas where imagination can soar. It pays homage to the exquisite art of cooking, where low-calorie Instructions becomes a kind of self-care that respects both the palette and the body. People who embark on this culinary trip will be immersed in a world where nutrition and flavor work in perfect harmony to create a symphony of flavor that will leave a lasting impression on the plate and the soul.

Developing low-calorie cottage cheese recipes requires a combination of imagination and practicality, and having the correct cooking tools may really improve your culinary experience. Here is a thorough list of kitchen tools that can help you create delectable and healthy dishes:

1. Blender or food processor: A necessary appliance for blending cottage cheese into sauces, dips, and smoothies to achieve smooth textures.

2. Fine mesh strainer or cheesecloth: For thickening cottage cheese into a consistency suitable for spreads and desserts by removing excess moisture.

3. Mixing Bowls: To blend, blend, and blend ingredients, various sized blending bowls are required.

4. A whisk: can be used to blend ingredients, whisk sauces, and produce smooth textures.

5. Measuring Cups and Spoons: To ensure portion control and preserve nutritional balance in low-calorie cooking, precise measurements are essential.

6. Spatulas: Rubber or silicone spatulas are great for folding ingredients, scraping bowls, and making sure that no delicious mixture is lost.

7. Chef's knife and cutting board: For slicing fruits, vegetables, and other materials, you must have a decent knife and a cutting board.

8. Grater: Used to grate fruits, vegetables, or even to flavorfully add a little cheese.

9. Oven safe baking utensils and dishes: For making baked goods like cheesecakes and casseroles.

10. Nonstick Skillet or Frying Pan: Perfect for sautéing foods without using a lot of oil.

11. Nonstick Cooking Spray: To lightly cover baking utensils and pans to prevent sticking while consuming less calories.

12. Oven mitts: These are necessary when handling hot cookware and plates.

13. Zester or Microplane: Used to finely grind items or add a blast of citrus zest.

14. Muffin tins: For baking baked goods or mini-quiches with portion management.

15. Hand or stand blender: Useful for blending together ingredients for desserts and generating creamy mixtures.

16. Salad Spinner: For effectively washing and drying greens for salads and other foods.

17. Steamer basket: Use this to steam veggies without adding too much oil.

18. Silicone molds: are fantastic for making individual dessert and pudding portions.

19. Plastic wrap or food storage containers: Leftovers, prepared components, and dishes that have been finished can all be stored using plastic wrap or food storage containers.

20. Citrus Juicer: Used to squeeze out fresh juice from citrus fruits to flavor food.

21. Fine Grain Sieve: Helps produce a smooth texture by straining and sifting ingredients.

The use of a rolling pin is necessary to make thin dough or crusts for dishes like low-calorie cheesecake.

23. Pastry Brush: Useful for sprinkling meals with thin layers of sauce or oil.

24. A timer or kitchen timer: is necessary for keeping track of cooking times correctly and avoiding overcooking.

With these cooking tools at your disposal, you can start your low-calorie cottage cheese cooking journey with confidence and experiment, produce, and enjoy a range of delectable and healthy recipes.

Low-calorie Breakfast Recipes

Here are low-calorie breakfast recipes using cottage cheese:

Cottage Cheese Pancakes:

Ingredients:

1/2 low-fat cottage cheese

2 eggs

Oats, rolled, 1/4 cup

1/2 teaspoon of vanilla extract

A quarter teaspoon of baking powder

Instructions:

1. In a blender, blend all ingredients and process until completely smooth.

2. To make pancakes, spoon tiny amounts of batter into a hot nonstick skillet.

3. Cook until surface bubbles appear, flip, and continue to cook until golden.

Cottage Cheese and Veggie Omelette:

Ingredients:

3 eggs

1/4 cup cottage cheese with low-fat

Veggies that have been chopped, such as spinach, tomatoes, bell peppers, onions, etc.

Pepper and salt as desired

Instructions:

1. Blend the eggs and cottage cheese in a bowl.

2. Sauté vegetables in a heated skillet with a little cooking spray.

3. After the egg mixture has been added, cook until set, fold it before serving.

Cottage Cheese Breakfast Burrito:

Ingredients:

Gluten free tortilla

1/4 cup cottage cheese with low-fat

Scrambled egg whites

Avocado slices

Salsa

Instructions:

1. Spread the tortilla with cottage cheese.

2. Add salsa, avocado slices, and scrambled egg whites to the layer.

3. Take a seat and enjoy.

Cottage Cheese Parfait:

Ingredients:

A half cup of low-fat cottage cheese

Strawberries, blueberries, and raspberries blended together

Honey for granola (optional)

Instructions:

1. In a glass, arrange the cottage cheese, berries, and granola.

2. Continue adding layers.

3. If desired, drizzle with honey.

Cottage Cheese Breakfast Bowl:

Ingredients:

A half cup of low-fat cottage cheese

Chopped banana

Chopped nuts (walnuts and almonds)

Cinnamon

Instructions:

1. Fill a bowl with cottage cheese.

2. Add banana slices, almonds, and a dash of cinnamon on top.

Cottage Cheese and Spinach Wrap:

Ingredients:

Wheat based wrap

1/4 cup cottage cheese with low-fat

Leafy baby spinach

Chicken or turkey breast sliced

Hummus or mustard

Instructions:

1. Cover the wrap with cottage cheese.

2. Add spinach and sliced meat to the layer.

3. Include a mustard or hummus spread.

4. Take a seat and enjoy.

Cottage Cheese Breakfast Quesadilla

Ingredients:

Gluten free tortilla

1/4 cup cottage cheese with low-fat

Chopped tomato

Fresh leaves of basil

Ingredients:

1. Cover one half of the tortilla with cottage cheese.

2. Add basil leaves and tomato slices to the layer.

3. Half fold the tortilla, then softly cook it until it turns golden.

Cottage Cheese and Veggie Toast:

Ingredients:

Pieces of whole grain bread

1/4 cup cottage cheese with low-fat

Cucumber slices

Chopped radish

Sprouts

Instructions:

1. On toasted slices of bread, spread cottage cheese.

2. Add cucumber, radish, and sprouts to the layer.

Cottage Cheese and Berries Smoothie:

Ingredients:

A half cup of low-fat cottage cheese

Berries in a blend (strawberries and blueberries)

Unsweetened almond milk

Ice cubes

Instructions:

1. Blend the following ingredients in a blender until smooth: cottage cheese, berries, almond milk, and ice cubes.

Cottage Cheese and Peanut Butter Toast:

Ingredients:

Slices of whole grain bread

1/4 cup cottage cheese with low-fat

Almond butter

Chopped banana

Instructions:

1. On toasted slices of bread, spread cottage cheese.

2. Top with banana slices and drizzle more peanut butter.

Cottage Cheese Breakfast Burrito Bowl:

Ingredients:

A half cup of low-fat cottage cheese

Scrambled egg whites

(Rinsed and canned) black beans

Salsa

Chopped coriander

Instructions:

1. Arrange black beans, cottage cheese, and scrambled egg whites in a bowl.

2. Add chopped cilantro and salsa on top.

Cottage Cheese and Tomato Open-faced:

Ingredients:

Slices of whole grain bread

1/4 cup cottage cheese with low-fat

Chopped tomato

Fresh leaves of basil

Instructions:

1. On toasted slices of bread, spread cottage cheese.

2. Add basil leaves and tomato slices to the layer.

Cottage Cheese and Apple Cinnamon:

Ingredients:

A half cup of low-fat cottage cheese

Apple slices

Cinnamon

Chopped almonds

Instructions:

1. In a glass, arrange the cottage cheese, apple slices, cinnamon, and chopped almonds.

Cottage Cheese and Veggie Breakfast:

Ingredients:

Wheat based wrap

1/4 cup cottage cheese with low-fat

Peppers, cut into slices

Red onion sliced

Baby spinach leaves

Instructions:

1. Cover the wrap with cottage cheese.

2. Add spinach, bell peppers, and red onions to the layer.

3. Take a seat and enjoy.

Cottage Cheese Stuffed Bell Peppers:

Ingredients:

Bell peppers seeded and split in half.

1/2 cup of low-fat cottage cheese

Spinach, chopped

Chopped tomatoes

(Optional) Low-fat shredded cheese

Instructions:

1. Blend the cottage cheese with the spinach and tomatoes.

2. Spoon the mixtures into the halves of bell peppers.

3. If desired, top with low-fat shredded cheese.

4. Bake peppers until they are soft.

Cottage Cheese and Chia Seed Pudding:

Ingredients:

A half cup of low-fat cottage cheese

Chia seeds, 2 tablespoons

Unsweetened almond milk

Vanilla flavoring

Fresh berries

Instructions:

1. Blend cottage cheese, almond milk, chia seeds, and vanilla essence.

2. Leave it in the fridge all night.

3. Before serving, garnish with fresh berries.

Cottage Cheese and Turkey Breakfast:

Ingredients:

Whole wheat wrap

1/4 cup cottage cheese with low-fat

Chicken or turkey breast sliced

Avocado slices

Baby spinach leaves

Instructions:

1. Spread cottage cheese on the wrap in Instructions.

2. Add spinach, avocado, and cut meat to the layer.

3. Take a seat and enjoy.

Cottage Cheese and Smoked Salmon Toast:

Ingredients:

Pieces of whole grain bread

1/4 cup cottage cheese with low-fat

Salmon smoked.

Cucumber slices

Fresh dill

Instructions:

1. On toasted slices of bread, spread cottage cheese.

2. Top with cucumber, smoked salmon, and fresh dill.

Cottage Cheese and Berry Parfait:

Ingredients:

A half cup of low-fat cottage cheese

Strawberries and raspberries blended together

Greek yogurt without sugar

An ice cube

Instructions:

1. Blend the Greek yogurt, cottage cheese, berries, and ice cubes until smooth.

Cottage Cheese and Pesto Breakfast Toast:

Ingredients:

Pieces of whole grain bread

1/4 cup cottage cheese with low-fat

Cherry tomatoes sliced with basil pesto

Instructions:

1. On toasted slices of bread, spread cottage cheese.

2. Add cherry tomatoes that have been thinly sliced and drizzle with basil pesto.

These inventive low-calorie cottage cheese breakfast recipes offer a variety of flavors and textures to help you start the day off right and feeling satisfied.

Have fun experimenting with these recipes and modifying them to your personal tastes

Smoothie Recipes

Here are tasty and healthy low-calorie cottage cheese smoothie recipes. These dishes are created to offer a healthy combination of protein, fiber, and vitamins that will keep you full and invigorated.

Fruit Blast:

Ingredients:

A half cup of low-fat cottage cheese

Strawberries, blueberries, and raspberries totaling 1/2 cup

1/2 banana

1/2 cup almond milk without sugar

An ice cube

Instructions:

Blend each item until it is smooth to prepare. The consistency of the almond milk can be adjusted.

Green Powerhouse:

Ingredients:

A half cup of low-fat cottage cheese

1 cup spinach

1/2 banana

1/4 avocado

1/2 cup coconut water or water

Fresh mint leaves, if desired

Ice cubes

Instructions:

Blend all ingredients until they are smooth and green throughout Instructions.

Tropical Delight:

Ingredients:

A half cup of low-fat cottage cheese

1/2 cup pieces of pineapple

1/2 banana

Greek yogurt, 1/4 cup

1/2 coconut water

Ice cubes

Instructions:

Blend all ingredients together till they have the flavor of the tropics.

Creamy Peanut Butter:

Ingredients:

A half cup of low-fat cottage cheese

A tbsp. of organic peanut butter

1/2 banana

1/2 cup almond milk without sugar

Ice cubes

Ingredients:

Blend all ingredients in a blender until they are creamy and peanut butter like.

Vanilla Almond Dream:

Ingredients:

A half cup of low-fat cottage cheese

1/2 teaspoon of vanilla extract

1/4 cup of almond slices

1/2 cup almond milk without sugar

Ice cubes

Instructions:

Blend each item until it is smooth and creamy.

Peachy Keen:

Ingredients:

A half cup of low-fat cottage cheese

1 pitted and thinly sliced peach

1/2 banana

1/2 cup coconut water or water

Ice cubes

Instructions:

Blend all ingredients together until they are peachy perfection.

Spinach Berry Fusion:

Ingredients:

A half cup of low-fat cottage cheese

1/2 blended berries

Handful of spinach

1/2 cup coconut water or water

Ice cubes

Instructions:

All components should be blended together to obtain the desired flavor fusion.

Mango Tango:

Ingredients:

A half cup of low-fat cottage cheese

1/2 cup pieces of mango

1/2 banana

1/2 cup coconut water or water

Ice cubes

Instructions:

To prepare, blend all ingredients and blend till a tropical tango is formed.

Coffee Kick:

Ingredients:

A half cup of low-fat cottage cheese

1/2 cup of cold brewed coffee

1/2 banana

1 tablespoon of unsweetened cocoa powder

1/2 cup almond milk without sugar

Ice cubes

Instructions:

Blend each ingredient until a caffeinated treat is produced.

Apple Cinnamon Spice:

Ingredients:

A half cup of low-fat cottage cheese

1/2 apple, sliced and cored

1/2 teaspoon of cinnamon

1/2 nutmeg teaspoon

1/2 cup almond milk without sugar

Ice cubes

Instructions:

The ingredients should be blended together to create a warm apple cinnamon blend.

Blueberry Basil Bliss:

Ingredients:

A half cup of low-fat cottage cheese

1/2 blueberries

Few fresh basil leaves

1/2 cup coconut water or water

Ice cubes

Instructions:

Blend all the ingredients till you get a blast of blueberry and basil delight.

Chocolate Banana Crunch:

Ingredients:

A half cup of low-fat cottage cheese

1/2 banana

1 tablespoon of unsweetened cocoa powder

Chia seeds, one tablespoon

1/4 cup of almonds, smashed

1/2 cup almond milk without sugar

Ice cubes

Instructions:

All ingredients should be blended to a chocolate crunch is reached.

Pumpkin Spice Smoothie:

Ingredients:

A half cup of low-fat cottage cheese

Canned pumpkin puree, 1/4 cup

1/2 banana

A half teaspoon of pumpkin pie spice

1/2 cup almond milk without sugar

Ice cubes

Instructions:

Blend all ingredients together to create a pumpkin spice.

Mixed Nuts Medley:

Ingredients:

A half cup of low-fat cottage cheese

Blended nuts (walnuts, almonds, and cashews) in 1/4 cup

1/2 banana

1/2 cup almond milk without sugar

Ice cubes

Instructions:

All ingredients should be blended together to create a nutty medley before serving.

Raspberry Lime Refresher:

Ingredients:

A half cup of low-fat cottage cheese

1/2 cup raspberries

1 lime juice

1/2 cup coconut water or water

Ice cubes

Instructions:

Blend all ingredients together to create a cool raspberrylime combo.

Carrot Cake Smoothie:

Ingredients:

A half cup of low-fat cottage cheese

1/2 cup of shredded carrots

1/2 banana

1/2 teaspoon of cinnamon

1/4 nutmeg teaspoon

1/2 cup almond milk without sugar

Ice cubes

Instructions:

Blend all ingredients together until you have a mixture that resembles carrot cake.

Lemon Berry Zest:

Ingredients:

A half cup of low-fat cottage cheese

A half cup of blended berries

Zest of 1 lemon

1/2 cup coconut water or water

Ice cubes

Instructions:

Blend all the ingredients together to create a zesty berry blend before serving.

Green Kiwi:

Ingredients:

A half cup of low-fat cottage cheese

1 sliced and peeled kiwi

Handful of spinach

1/2 cup coconut water or water

Ice cubes

Instructions:

All ingredients should be blended together to create a kiwigreen delight.

Oats Raisin Smoothie:

Ingredients:

A half cup of low-fat cottage cheese

Oats, rolled, 1/4 cup

1 cup of raisins

1/2 teaspoon of cinnamon

1/2 teaspoon of vanilla extract

1/2 cup almond milk without sugar

Ice cubes

Instructions:

To make oatmeal raisin pleasure, blend all ingredients in a blender.

Cucumber Mint Refresh:

Ingredients:

A half cup of low-fat cottage cheese

1/2 Sliced and peeled cucumber

A few fresh mint leaves

1/2 cup coconut water or water

Ice cubes

Instructions:

Make a refreshing cucumber-mint beverage by blending all the ingredients together.

In order to keep your taste buds piqued while prioritizing health and wellness, low-calorie cottage cheese smoothie recipes come in a variety of tastes and textures.

As you begin your cooking adventure, feel free to alter ingredients to suit your dietary preferences and try out new combinations.

Dessert Recipes

Here are low-calorie cottage cheese dessert recipes that are filling and healthy:

Chocolate Protein Pudding:

Ingredients:

1 cup cottage cheese with low-fat

2 tablespoons chocolate powder, unsweetened

1 tablespoon maple syrup or honey

Instructions:

To prepare, combine cottage cheese with the sweetener and chocolate powder in a blender. Before serving, chill in the refrigerator.

Lemon Cottage Cheese Bars:

Ingredients:

1 cup cottage cheese with low-fat

1/4 cup lemon juice

One lemon zest

2 teaspoons of agave syrup or honey

Instructions:

To prepare, combine the cottage cheese, sugar, and lemon juice. Pour into a tiny baking dish, and then chill until firm. Slice into bars, and then serve.

Vanilla Cottage Cheese Dip:

Ingredients:

1 cup cottage cheese with low-fat

1 teaspoon of vanilla extract

1 tablespoon of powdered stevia or other preferred sweetener

Instructions:

To make the dish, combine the cottage cheese, sugar, and vanilla extract in a creamy blender. Serve with fruit slices.

Cottage Cheese Fruit Salad:

Ingredients:

1 cup cottage cheese with low-fat

1 cup of assorted fruits, such as melon, grapes, and kiwis.

1 tablespoon of mint leaves, chopped

Instructions:

To prepare, blend cottage cheese with the fruit mixture. Cut mint leaves for garnish.

Cottage Cheese and Banana Bowl:

Ingredients:

1/2 cup cottage cheese with low-fat

1 thinly sliced tiny ripe banana

1 tablespoon of organic peanut butter

Instructions:

To prepare, put the cottage cheese in a bowl, add the banana slices, and then sprinkle the peanut butter over everything.

Cinnamon Apple Cottage Cheese Bowl:

Ingredients:

1/2 cup cottage cheese with low-fat

1 sliced tiny apple

1/2 teaspoon of ground cinnamon,

Instructions:

To prepare, mix together the cottage cheese, apple, and cinnamon. Mix thoroughly, and then enjoy.

Cottage Cheese Chocolate Mousse:

Ingredients:

1 cup cottage cheese with low-fat

2 tablespoons chocolate powder, unsweetened

1 tablespoon agave nectar or honey

Instructions:

To prepare, combine cottage cheese with the sweetener and chocolate powder in a blender. Before serving, place in the fridge for a few hours.

Raspberry Cottage Cheese Parfait:

Ingredients:

1/2 cup cottage cheese with low-fat

Fresh raspberries, 1/2 cup

1 tablespoon of almonds, crushed

Instructions:

To assemble, fill a glass with cottage cheese, raspberries, and ground almonds. Enjoy the layers again and again.

Cottage cheese with honey and walnuts:

Ingredients:

1/2 cup cottage cheese with low-fat

1 teaspoon finely chopped walnuts

1 teaspoon of honey

Instructions:

To prepare, combine honey, cottage cheese, and chopped walnuts. As a dessert or a snack, serve.

Cottage Cheese Fruit Pizza:

Ingredients:

1 whole-wheat pita or tortilla

1/2 cup cottage cheese with low-fat

A variety of sliced fruits, including strawberries, kiwis, and bananas.

Instructions:

Cover the tortilla or pita with cottage cheese. Sliced fruits should be placed on top.

Mango Coconut Cottage Cheese Delight:

Ingredients:

1/2 cup cottage cheese with low-fat

1/2 ripe diced mango

2 tablespoons of coconut meat.

Instructions:

To prepare, mix together the cottage cheese, mango, and coconut. Mix thoroughly, and then enjoy.

Blueberry Lemon Cottage Cheese Bowl:

Ingredients:

1/2 cup cottage cheese with low-fat

1/4 cup blueberries

1 lemon zest

Instructions:

Mix cottage cheese, blueberries, and lemon zest in a bowl. As a cool dessert, serve.

Almond butter chocolate dip:

Ingredients:

1/2 cup cottage cheese with low-fat

1 teaspoon of almond butter

1 teaspoon cocoa powder, unsweetened

Instructions:

Cottage cheese, almond butter, and cocoa powder should be thoroughly blended before serving. Dunk in your preferred fruits.

Strawberry Shortcake Parfait:

Ingredients:

1/2 cup cottage cheese with low-fat

A serving of sliced strawberries

1 crumbled wholegrain biscuit

Instructions:

To make, fill a glass with cottage cheese, sliced strawberries, and crumbled biscuit. Enjoy the mixture again and again.

Peach Melba Cottage Cheese Bowl:

Ingredients:

1/2 cup cottage cheese with low-fat

1 sliced ripe peach

A few freshly picked raspberries

Instructions:

To prepare, combine the cottage cheese, raspberries, and diced peach. Enjoy the tastes while mixing slowly.

Chocolate Banana Cottage Cheese Shake:

Ingredients:

1/2 cup cottage cheese with low-fat

A single ripe banana

1 tablespoon chocolate powder, unsweetened

1/2 cup almond milk that is unsweetened

Instructions:

To make, combine almond milk, cottage cheese, banana, and cocoa powder in a blender until well combined. Savor as a smooth shake.

Coconut Lime Cottage Cheese Parfait:

Ingredients:

1/2 cup cottage cheese with low-fat

1 tablespoon of coconut shavings

1 lime's juice and zest

Instructions:

To prepare, combine cottage cheese, coconut shreds, lime juice, and zest. Serve in ramekins or little cups.

Blackberry Mint Cottage Cheese Parfait:

Ingredients:

1/2 cup cottage cheese with low-fat

Fresh blackberries, 1/2 cup

1 tablespoon of freshly chopped mint leaves

Instructions:

To prepare, fill a glass with cottage cheese, blackberries, and finely chopped mint. Enjoy the mixture again and again.

Vanilla Berry Cottage Cheese Bowl:

Ingredients:

1/2 cup cottage cheese with low-fat

1/2 cup of mixed berries (strawberries, blueberries, and raspberries)

A half teaspoon of vanilla extract

Instructions:

To prepare, combine the cottage cheese, vanilla extract, and mixed berries. Gently combine, and then enjoy the sweetness.

These delicious low-calorie cottage cheese dessert recipes have a variety of tastes and textures, giving you a mouthwatering selection of dishes to sate your sweet need without jeopardizing your fitness objectives.

Experiment with these dishes to your heart's content and relish the delicious flavors they bring to your table.

Juice Recipes

Here are low-calorie cottage cheese juice recipes with serving sizes:

Citrus Creamsicle Cooler:

Ingredients:

A half cup of cottage cheese

Orange juice, 1 cup

A teaspoon of lime juice

1/2 teaspoon of vanilla extract

(Optional) honey to taste

Instructions:

Blend each item until it is completely smooth. Serve chilled.

Berry Blast Refresher:

Ingredients:

A half cup of cottage cheese

1 cup of blended berries; Strawberry, blueberry, and raspberry.

1 cup pieces of watermelon

Fresh mint leaves

Instructions:

Blend cottage cheese, watermelon, and a variety of berries. Leafy mint is a nice garnish.

Tropical Pineapple Elixir:

Ingredients:

A half cup of cottage cheese

Pineapple juice, 1 cup

1/2 cup coconut water

Slices of kiwi

Instructions:

Coconut water, pineapple juice, and cottage cheese should be blended. Add slices of kiwi.

Green Veggie Reviver:

Ingredients:

A half cup of cottage cheese

1 chopped and peeled cucumber

Handful of spinach leaves

2 chopped celery stalks

Juice of 1 lemon

Fresh parsley

Instructions:

Blend each item until it is completely smooth. Add parsley as a garnish.

Apple Cinnamon Comfort:

Ingredients:

A half cup of cottage cheese

Apple juice, 1 cup

1/2 teaspoon of cinnamon

Nutmeg, just a pinch

Instructions:

Blend each component thoroughly. Add a cinnamon stick to the dish.

Beetroot Berry Fusion:

Ingredients:

A half cup of cottage cheese

Beet juice, 1 cup

1 cup of blueberries and raspberries blended together

Splash of lemon juice

Instructions:

To achieve the correct consistency, blend all components. Offer chilled.

Carrot Ginger Elixir:

Ingredients:

A half cup of cottage cheese

Carrot juice, 1 cup

Freshly grated ginger

Zest of 1 orange

Instructions:

All items should be thoroughly blended. Offer chilled.

Mango Peach Cream:

Ingredients:

A half cup of cottage cheese

Mango juice, 1 cup

Sliced peaches

1 lime juice

Instructions:

Mango juice, lime juice, and cottage cheese should be blended. Add slices of peach.

Pomegranate Cherry Delight:

Ingredients:

A half cup of cottage cheese

Pomegranate juice in a cup

Handful of pitted cherries

Splash of lime juice

Instructions:

Blend each item until it is completely smooth. Enjoy it chilled.

Herb-Infused Greens:

Ingredients:

A half cup of cottage cheese

Handful of spinach leaves

Handful of kale leaves

1 chopped and peeled cucumber

Handful of basil leaves

Juice of 1 lemon

Instructions:

Blend each item until it is completely smooth. Strain if desired.

Cucumber Mint Quencher:

Ingredients:

A half cup of cottage cheese

1 chopped and peeled cucumber

Fresh mint leaves

Juice of 1 lemon

Instructions:

Blend each item until it is completely smooth. Serve chilled.

Blueberry Lavender Serenity:

Ingredients:

A half cup of cottage cheese

Blueberry juice, 1 cup

Pinch of edible lavender buds

(Optional) honey to taste

Instructions:

Blend cottage cheese, blueberry juice, lavender buds, and honey.

Gingered Pear Pleasure:

Ingredients:

A half cup of cottage cheese

1 cup of pear juice

Grated fresh ginger

Juice from 1 lemon

Instructions:

To achieve the correct consistency, blend all components. Offer chilled.

Cranberry Mint Zest:

Ingredients:

A half cup of cottage cheese

Cranberry juice, 1 cup

Fresh mint leaves

Zest of 1 orange

Instructions:

Mint leaves, cottage cheese, and cranberry juice should be blended.
Add orange zest.

Watermelon Basil Bliss:

Ingredients:

A half cup of cottage cheese

Watermelon juice, 1 cup

Fresh leaves of basil

1 lime's juice

Instructions:

Blend each item until it is completely smooth. Add a basil sprig as
a garnish.

Turmeric Carrot Dream:

Ingredients:

A half cup of cottage cheese

Carrot juice, 1 cup

Pinch of turmeric powder

(Optional) Honey to taste

Instructions:

To prepare, blend cottage cheese, carrot juice, turmeric powder, and any more honey you'd like.

Strawberry Mint Refresher:

Ingredients:

A half cup of cottage cheese

Strawberry juice, 1 cup

Fresh mint leaves

Juice of 1 lemon

Instructions:

Strawberry juice, cottage cheese, and mint leaves should be blended. Serve chilled.

Lemon Ginger Detox:

Ingredients:

A half cup of cottage cheese

Juice of 2 lemons

Grated fresh ginger

Slices of cucumber

Instructions:

Blend each item until it is completely smooth. Strain if desired.

Pineapple Basil Breeze:

Ingredients:

A half cup of cottage cheese

Pineapple juice, 1 cup

Fresh leaves of basil

Juice of 1 lemon

Instructions:

Blend cottage cheese, lime juice, pineapple juice, and basil leaves. Offer chilled.

Minty Melon Refresher:

Ingredients:

A half cup of cottage cheese

1 cup of cantaloupe juice

Pieces of honeydew melon

Frcsh mint leaves

Instructions:

Honeydew pieces, cottage cheese, cantaloupe juice, and mint leaves should all be blended. Enjoy it chilled.

You are welcome to modify the component amounts to suit your personal tastes and serving requirements. Enjoy these inventive and hydrating cottage cheese juice recipes that are low in calories

Salad Recipes

Here are low-calorie cottage cheese salad recipes with measurements for all the ingredients and steps for making them:

Mediterranean Chickpea Salad with Cottage Cheese:

Ingredients:

1/2 cup low-fat cottage cheese

1 cup cooked chickpeas

1/4 cup sliced cucumber

1/2 cup cherry tomatoes

1/4 cup red onion, chopped

2 tbsp. freshly chopped parsley

Extra virgin olive oil, 1 tablespoon

1 tablespoon lemon juice

Pepper and salt as desired

Instructions:

Blend the chickpeas, cottage cheese, tomatoes, cucumber, red onion, and parsley in a big bowl. Blend the lemon juice and olive oil in a small bowl. Salt and pepper the salad then drizzle over the dressing and gently toss to blend.

Berry Spinach Cottage Cheese Salad:

Ingredients:

2 cups of baby spinach

1/2 cup cottage cheese with low-fat

Berries mixed of strawberries, blueberries, and raspberries, 1/2 cup

A cup of chopped almonds

Balsamic vinegar, 1 tablespoon

1 teaspoon of honey

Instructions:

Put spinach in a serving dish. Cottage cheese and blended berries go on top. Almonds, diced, should be sprinkled on top.

Blend honey and balsamic vinegar in a small bowl. Immediately prior to serving, drizzle over the salad.

Greek Cottage Cheese Salad:

Ingredients:

1 cup cottage cheese with low-fat

1/2 cup cucumbers, diced

1/4 cup chopped Kalamata olives,

1/4 cup sliced red onion, and

1/2 cup diced tomatoes

2 tbsps. of feta cheese, crumbled

1 tbsp. freshly chopped dill

1tablespoon lemon juice

Pepper and salt as desired

Instructions:

Cottage cheese, cucumber, tomatoes, red onion, olives, feta cheese, and dill should all be blended in a bowl. Add salt and pepper, drizzle with lemon juice, and gently toss to blend.

Zesty Corn and Cottage Cheese Salad:

Ingredients:

Cooked corn kernels, 1 cup

1/2 cup cottage cheese with low-fat

1/2 cup red bell peppers, chopped

1/4 cup freshly chopped cilantro

2 tbsps. Lime juice

1 tablespoon chopped Jalapeno (optional)

Pepper and salt as desired

Instructions:

Corn, cottage cheese, red bell pepper, cilantro, and jalapeno are all blended in a bowl. Add salt and pepper; drizzle with lime juice, and gently blend to blend.

Caprese Cottage Cheese Salad:

Ingredients:

1 cup cottage cheese with low-fat

1/2 cup of cherry tomatoes

1 cup of fresh mozzarella balls

1 cup of torn fresh basil leaves

2 tablespoons of balsamic glaze

Pepper and salt as desired

Instructions:

Cottage cheese, cherry tomatoes, mozzarella balls, and basil leaves should all be blended gently in a bowl. Add salt and pepper, drizzle with balsamic glaze, and gently toss to blend.

Grilled Vegetables Cottage Cheese Salad:

Ingredients:

1 cup of grilled blended veggies, including eggplant, bell peppers, and zucchini

1/2 cup cottage cheese with little fat

2 tbsps. freshly chopped parsley

1tablespoon lemon juice

1 teaspoon olive oil

Pepper and salt as desired

Instructions:

In a bowl, blend the grilled veggies with the cottage cheese, parsley, lemon juice, and olive oil. Add salt and pepper, and then gently toss to blend.

Asian-Inspired Cottage Cheese Slaw:

Ingredients:

1 cup of cabbage, chopped

1/4 cup of shredded carrots and

1/2 cup of low-fat cottage cheese

Green onions, chopped, 2 tablespoons

2 tablespoons of rice vinegar

Low sodium soy sauce, 1 tablespoon

1 teaspoon sesame oil

1/2 tbsp. freshly grated ginger

Instructions:

Cabbage, cottage cheese, carrots, and green onions are all blended in a bowl. Rice vinegar, soy sauce, sesame oil, and grated ginger should all be blended in a different bowl. Over the slaw, drizzle the dressing, and gently toss to blend.

Southwest Cottage Cheese Salad:

Ingredients:

1 cup cottage cheese with low-fat

1/2 cup rinsed and drained black beans

1/4 cup chopped red onion and

2 cups of cooked corn kernels

1/4 cup red bell peppers, chopped

2 tbsps. freshly chopped cilantro

1 tbsp. of lime juice

1/2 teaspoon ground cumin

Pepper and salt as desired

Instructions:

Cottage cheese, black beans, corn, red onion, red bell pepper, cilantro, and a bowl. Blend lime juice and ground cumin in a small bowl. Salt and pepper to taste, then drizzle over the salad and gently toss to blend.

Tuna and Cottage Cheese Salad:

Ingredients:

1 cup cottage cheese with low-fat

1 can (5 Oz) flaked and drained tuna

1/2 cup cucumbers, diced

1/4 cup red onion, chopped

2 tbsps. freshly chopped parsley

1tablespoon lemon juice

Dijon mustard, 1 teaspoon

Pepper and salt as desired

Instructions:

Cottage cheese, tuna, cucumber, red onion, and parsley should all be blended in a bowl. Blend lemon juice and Dijon mustard in a small bowl. Salt and pepper to taste, then drizzle over the salad and gently toss to blend.

Quinoa and Cottage Cheese Salad:

Ingredients:

1 cup of cooked quinoa

1/2 cup of low-fat cottage cheese.

1/2 cup cucumbers, diced

1/4 cup red bell peppers, chopped

Chopped fresh parsley, 1/4 cup

2 tbsps. Lemon juice

Extra virgin olive oil, 1 tablespoon

Pepper and salt as desired

Instructions:

Cucumber, red bell pepper, cottage cheese, parsley, and cooked quinoa should all be blended in a bowl. Add salt and pepper, drizzle with olive oil and lemon juice, and gently toss to incorporate.

Apple Walnuts Cottage Cheese Salad:

Ingredients:

1 cup cottage cheese with low-fat

1 diced apple

1/4 cup chopped walnuts

2 tbsp. dried cranberries

1/2 tbsp. cinnamon

1 tbsp. honey

Instructions:

In a bowl, blend cottage cheese, chopped apple, walnuts, and dried cranberries. Sprinkle with cinnamon and drizzle with honey. Gently blend by tossing.

Beet and Cottage Cheese Salad:

Ingredients:

1 cup of beets, boiled and diced

1/2 cup cottage cheese with low-fat

Chopped fresh mint, 1/4 cup

2 tablespoons chopped pistachios

Balsamic vinegar, 1 tablespoon

1 teaspoon of honey

Instructions:

Cooked beets, cottage cheese, mint, and pistachios should all be blended in a bowl. Blend honey and balsamic vinegar in a small bowl. Toss the salad lightly to incorporate after drizzling over it.

Avocado and Cottage Cheese Salad:

Ingredients:

1 cup cottage cheese with low-fat

1 diced avocado and

1/2 cup diced cucumber

1/4 cup red onion, chopped

2 tbsps. freshly chopped cilantro

1 tbsp. of lime juice

Pepper and salt as desired

Instructions:

Cottage cheese, diced avocado, cucumber, red onion, and cilantro should all be blended gently in a bowl. Add salt and pepper; drizzle with lime juice, and gently blend to blend.

Roasted Veggie Cottage Cheese Salad:

Ingredients:

1 cup of roasted blended veggies, including cauliflower, broccoli, and sweet potatoes

1/2 cup cottage cheese with low-fat

2 tbsp. freshly chopped thyme

1tablespoon lemon juice

1 teaspoon olive oil

Pepper and salt as desired

Instructions:

In a bowl, blend cottage cheese, thyme, lemon juice, and olive oil with the roasted veggies. Add salt and pepper, and then gently toss to blend.

Spinach and Cottage Cheese Salad with Orange Vinaigrette:

Ingredients:

2 cups of baby spinach

1/2 cup cottage cheese with low-fat

Sliced orange in half

2 tbsps. of chopped pecans

1 tablespoon orange juice

1 tablespoon of olive oil

1 teaspoon of honey

Pepper and salt as desired

Instructions:

Put spinach in a serving dish. Orange segments, cottage cheese, and chopped pecans should be added on top. Blend orange juice, olive oil, honey, salt, and pepper in a small bowl. Immediately prior to serving, drizzle over the salad.

Cucumber Avocado and Cottage Cheese Salad:

Ingredients:

1 cup cottage cheese with low- fat

1 diced cucumber

1 diced avocado

2 tbsp. finely chopped fresh mint

1tablespoon lemon juice

1 teaspoon olive oil

Pepper and salt as desired

Instructions:

Cottage cheese, chopped cucumber, diced avocado, and mint should all be blended gently in a bowl. Add salt and pepper, drizzle with olive oil and lemon juice, and gently toss to incorporate.

Cranberries Pecan Cottage Cheese Salad:

Ingredients:

1/4 cup dried cranberries,

1/4 cup chopped pecans, and

1 cup low-fat cottage cheese

2 tbsps. freshly chopped parsley

Balsamic vinegar, 1 tablespoon

1 teaspoon of honey

Instructions:

In a bowl, blend cottage cheese, pecans, dried cranberries, and parsley. Blend honey and balsamic vinegar in a small bowl. Toss the salad lightly to incorporate after drizzling over it.

Summer Corn and Cottage Cheese Salad:

Ingredients:

Cooked corn kernels, 1 cup

1/2 cup cottage cheese with low-fat

1/2 cup red bell peppers, chopped

1/4 cup finely minced fresh basil

Red wine vinegar, 2 tablespoons

Extra virgin olive oil, 1 tablespoon

Pepper and salt as desired

Instructions:

Cooked corn, cottage cheese, red bell pepper, and basil should all be blended in a bowl. Blend red wine vinegar and olive oil in a small bowl. Salt and pepper to taste, then drizzle over the salad and gently toss to blend.

Broccoli Cottage Cheese Salad:

Ingredients:

1 cup of broccoli florets, steamed

1/2 cup low-fat cottage cheese

1/4 cup red onion, chopped

2 tbsps. freshly cut chives

1 tablespoon lemon juice

Dijon mustard, 1 teaspoon

Pepper and salt as desired

Instructions:

In a bowl, blend the cottage cheese, red onion, chives, and steamed broccoli. Blend lemon juice and Dijon mustard in a small bowl. Salt and pepper to taste, then drizzle over the salad and gently toss to blend.

Peach and Cottage Cheese Salad:

Ingredients:

1 cup cottage cheese with low-fat

1 ripe sliced peach

1/4 cup of chopped, toasted almonds

2 tbsp. finely chopped fresh mint

1 tablespoon of honey

Vanilla extract, 1/2 tsp.

Instructions:

Slices of peach, cottage cheese, roasted almonds, and mint should all be blended gently in a bowl. Add vanilla extract and honey, then gently blend to blend.

Mango Salsa Cottage Cheese Salad:

Ingredients:

1 cup cottage cheese with low-fat

1 chopped ripe mango,

1/4 cup diced red onion,

1/2 cup diced red bell pepper

2 tbsps. freshly chopped cilantro

1 tbsp. of lime juice

1/2 teaspoon chili powder

Pepper and salt as desired

Instructions:

Cottage cheese, chopped mango, red bell pepper, red onion, and cilantro should all be blended gently in a bowl. Add salt and pepper, drizzle with lime juice, sprinkle with chili powder, and gently blend to blend.

Watermelon and Feta Cottage Cheese Salad:

Ingredients:

1 cup cottage cheese with low-fat

1 cup watermelon, diced, and

1/4 cup feta cheese, crumbled

2 tbsp. finely chopped fresh mint

Balsamic vinegar, 1 tablespoon

1 teaspoon of honey

Instructions:

Cottage cheese, chopped watermelon, feta cheese, and mint should all be blended in a bowl. Blend honey and balsamic vinegar in a small bowl. Toss the salad lightly to incorporate after drizzling over it.

Feel free to play around with these recipes, modify them to suit your preferences, and savor a variety of wholesome salads.

Conclusion

Low-calorie cottage cheese recipes appear as a bright tapestry of culinary exploration, where flavor dances with nutrition in a delicate symphony, blending health and delight. These recipes disprove the idea that eating healthily equates to deprivation and show that every dish can be a masterpiece of flavor and wellbeing.

Low-calorie cottage cheese dishes showcase the culinary prowess of people who cherish their palates and overall welfare. They range from the savory to the sweet, the straightforward to the complicated. We enjoy the delicate balance between the satisfying benefits of eating foods high in protein and the pleasure of savoring each morsel with each bite.

This culinary adventure honors both the adaptability of cottage cheese and the dish creators' limitless creativity. It's a celebration of the remarkable heights to which even the most common ingredients may be brought, nourishing our bodies and arousing our senses.

Low-calorie cottage cheese recipes fill the void in a world where flavor and health are sometimes presented as mutually exclusive concepts. They provide a fascinating synthesis that has no bounds.

They encourage us to reconsider our connection with food, to view the kitchen as a platform for expressing ourselves in a healthy way, and to enjoy the results of our inventive cooking.

Let's embrace the transformative power of low-calorie cottage cheese recipes as we set out on this tasty journey, not just as a way to fuel our bodies but also as a kind of creativity that feeds our souls.

These recipes help us to gain a fresh understanding of the close relationship between the food we make and the lives we lead, encouraging a way of living that is both scrumptiously enjoyable and profoundly nutritious.

Made in United States
Troutdale, OR
04/15/2025